PROVERB WISDOM

Navigating life wisely with 400+ quotes across 30+ topics from the Biblical book of Proverbs

By ML James

AUDIOBOOK OFFER

If you are new to Audible you can get the audiobook version of this book free with a free 30 days Audible trial.

Please follow the below *bit.ly* links based on where you reside.

US: *bit.ly/MLJ_Proverbs_US*

UK: *bit.ly/MLJ_Proverbs_UK*

France: *bit.ly/MLJ_Proverbs_FR*

Germany: *bit.ly/MLJ_Proverbs_DE*

All other countries: *bit.ly/MLJ_Proverbs_Others*

TABLE OF CONTENTS

INTRODUCTION

"Get good advice and you will succeed. Don't go charging into battle without a plan." Proverbs 20:18

- Seeking insights for living life wisely?
- Interested in learning ancient time-tested wisdom?
- Know someone who might benefit from this?

This Christian wisdom literature contains 400+ quotes of wisdom across 30+ topics from the Biblical book of Proverbs that's great for anyone interested in living wisely.

This book of wisdom will empower, inspire & steer you to do so through:

- Wisdom and instructions in wise dealing.
- Discerning the words of understanding.
- Giving shrewdness to the inexperienced.
- Knowledge and discretion to the young.
- Attaining sound counsel.
- Understanding proverbs and parables, the words and riddles of the wise.

Get ready to see your life transform over time as you learn & apply the divine wisdom!

DEDICATION

This book is dedicated to my dad.

Dad's been my rock, speaking words of love & wisdom into my life. His words & life inspires, guides and directs my path.

Dad's encouragement to study the Biblical book of Proverbs has lead me to write this book.

I love you dad.

THE 30 WISE SAYINGS

Listen and I will teach you what wise men have said. Study their teachings and you will be glad if you remember them and can quote them. I want you to put your trust in the Lord; that is why I am going to tell them to you now. I have written down thirty sayings for you. They contain knowledge and good advice and will teach you what the truth really is. Then when you are sent to find it out, you will bring back the right answer.

1. *Don't take advantage of the poor just because you can; don't take advantage of those who stand helpless in court. The Lord will argue their case for them and threaten the life of anyone who threatens theirs.*
2. *Don't make friends with people who have hot, violent tempers. You might learn their habits and not be able to change.*
3. *Don't promise to be responsible for someone else's debts. If you should be unable to pay, they will take away even your bed.*
4. *Never move an old boundary-mark that your ancestors established.*
5. *Show me a man who does a good job and I will show you a man who is better than most and worthy of the company of kings.*
6. *When you sit down to eat with an important man, keep in mind who he is. If you have a big appetite, restrain yourself. Don't be greedy for the fine food he serves; he may be trying to trick you.*

7.   Be wise enough not to wear yourself out trying to get rich. Your money can be gone in a flash, as if it had grown wings and flown away like an eagle.

8.   Don't eat at the table of a stingy man or be greedy for the fine food he serves. "Come on and have more", he says, but he really doesn't mean it. What he really thinks is what he really is. You will vomit up whatever you have eaten, and all your flattery will be wasted.

9.   Don't try to talk sense to a fool; he can't appreciate it.

10.   Never move an old boundary mark or take over land owned by orphans. The Lord is their powerful defender and will argue their case against you.

11.   Pay attention to your teacher and learn all you can.

12.   Don't hesitate to discipline a child. A good spanking won't kill him. As a matter of fact, it might save his life.

13.   Son, if you become wise, I will be very happy. I will be proud when I hear you speaking words of wisdom.

14.   Don't be envious of sinful people; let the reverence for the Lord be the concern of your life. If it is, you have a bright future.

15.   Listen, my son, be wise and give serious thought to the way you live. Don't associate with people who drink too much wine or stuff themselves with food. Drunkards and gluttons will be reduced to poverty. If all you do is eat and sleep; you will soon be wearing rags.

16.   Listen to your father; without him you would not exist. When your mother is old, show her your appreciation. Truth, wisdom, learning, and good sense-these are worth paying for, but too valuable for you to sell. A righteous man's father has good reason

to be happy. You can take pride in a wise son. Make your father and mother proud of you; give your mother that happiness.

17.   *Pay close attention, my son, and let my life be your example. Prostitutes and immoral women are a deadly trap. They wait for you like robbers and cause many men to be unfaithful.*

18.   *Show me someone who drinks too much, who has to try out some new drink, and I will show someone miserable and sorry for himself, always causing trouble and always complaining. His eyes are bloodshot and he has bruises that could have been avoided. Don't let wine tempt you, even though it is rich red, though it sparkles in the cup and goes down smoothly. The next morning you will feel like as if you have been bitten by a poisonous snake. Weird sights will appear before your eyes and you will not be able to think or speak clearly. You will feel as if you were out on the ocean, sea-sick, swinging high up in the rigging of a tossing ship. "I must have been hit", you will say; "I must have been beaten up but I don't remember it. Why can't I wake up? I need another drink."*

19.   *Don't be envious of evil people and don't try to make friends with them. Causing trouble is all they ever think about; every time they open their mouth someone is going to get hurt.*

20.   *Homes are built on the foundation of wisdom and understanding. Where there is knowledge, the rooms are furnished with valuable, beautiful things.*

21.   *Being wise is better than being strong; yes, knowledge is more important than strength. After all, you must*

make careful plans before you fight a battle, and the more advice you get, the more likely you are to win.

22. *Wise sayings are too deep for a stupid person to understand. He has nothing to say when important matters are being discussed.*

23. *If you are always planning evil, you will earn a reputation as a troublemaker. Any scheme a fool thinks up is sinful. People hate a person who has nothing but scorn for others.*

24. *If you are weak in a crisis; you are weak indeed.*

25. *Don't hesitate to rescue someone who is about to be executed unjustly. You may say that it is none of your business, but God knows and judges your motives. He keeps watch on you; he knows. And he will reward you according to what you do.*

26. *Son, eat honey; it is good. And just as honey from the comb is sweet on your tongue, you may be sure that wisdom is good for the soul. Get wisdom and you have a bright future.*

27. *Don't be like the wicked who scheme to rob an honest man or to take away his home. No matter how often an honest man falls, he always gets up again; but disaster destroys the wicked.*

28. *Don't be glad when your enemy meets disaster and don't rejoice when he stumbles. The Lord will know if you are gloating and he will not like it; and then he might not punish him.*

29. *Don't let evil people worry you; don't be envious of them. A wicked person has no future-nothing to look forward to.*

30. *Have reverence for the Lord, my son, and honour the king. Have nothing to do with people who rebel against them; such men could be ruined in a moment.*

Do you realize the disaster that God or the king can cause?

PROVERBS 22:17-22

MORE WISE SAYINGS

Wise men have also said these things:

1. *It is wrong for a judge to be prejudiced. If he pronounces a guilty person innocent, he will be cursed and hated by everyone. Judges who punish the guilty, however, will be prosperous and enjoy a good reputation.*
2. *An honest answer is a sign of true friendship.*
3. *Don't build your house and establish a home until your fields are ready and you are sure that you can earn a living.*
4. *Don't give evidence against someone else without good reason, or say misleading things about him. Don't say, "I'll do to him just what he did to me! I'll get even with him!"*
5. *I walked through the fields and vineyards of a lazy, stupid man. They were full of thorn bushes and overgrown with weeds. The stone wall around them had fallen down. I looked at this, thought about it, and learned a lesson from it: Have a nap and sleep if you want to. Fold your hands and rest awhile, but while you are asleep, poverty will attack you like an armed robber.*

PROVERBS 24:23-34

LEARNING

He who gets wisdom loves his own soul. He who keeps understanding shall find good.

PROVERBS 19:8

Listen to counsel and receive instruction that you may be wise in your latter end.

PROVERBS 19:20

If you stop listening to instruction, my son, you will stray from the words of knowledge.

PROVERBS 19:27

Apply your heart to instruction and your ears to the words of knowledge.

PROVERBS 23:12

Buy the truth, and do not sell it. Get wisdom, discipline, and understanding.

PROVERBS 23:23

Iron sharpens iron; so a man sharpens his friend's countenance.

PROVERBS 27:17

GETTING ADVICE

The wise in heart accept commandments but a chattering fool will fall.

PROVERBS 10:8

Whoever despises instruction will pay for it but he who respects a command will be rewarded.

PROVERBS 13:13

A scoffer doesn't love to be reproved; he will not go to the wise.

PROVERBS 15:12

Where there is no counsel, plans fail; but in a multitude of counselors they are established.

PROVERBS 15:22

Listen to counsel and receive instruction that you may be wise in your latter end.

PROVERBS 19:20

Plans are established by advice; by wise guidance you wage war.

PROVERBS 20:18

A wise man has great power; and a knowledgeable man increases strength; for by wise guidance you wage your war; and victory is in many advisors.

PROVERBS 24:5-6

Take away the wicked from the king's presence and his throne will be established in righteousness.

PROVERBS 25:5

As an earring of gold and an ornament of fine gold so is a wise reprover to an obedient ear.

PROVERBS 25:12

THE POWER OF WORDS

My son, attend to my words. Turn your ear to my sayings. Let them not depart from your eyes. Keep them in the midst of your heart. For they are life to him who finds them, and health to all of his body.

PROVERBS 4:20-22

The mouth of the righteous is a spring of life but violence covers the mouth of the wicked.

PROVERBS 10:11

The lips of the righteous feed many but the foolish die for lack of understanding.

PROVERBS 10:21

The mouth of the righteous brings forth wisdom but the perverse tongue will be cut off. The lips of the righteous know what is acceptable but the mouth of the wicked is perverse.

PROVERBS 10:31-32

The words of the wicked are about lying in wait for blood but the speech of the upright rescues them.

PROVERBS 12:6

An evil man is trapped by sinfulness of lips but the righteous shall come out of trouble. A man shall be satisfied with good by the fruit of his mouth. The work of a man's hands shall be rewarded to him.

PROVERBS 12:13-14

There is one who speaks rashly like the piercing of a sword but the tongue of the wise heals.

PROVERBS 12:18

Anxiety in a man's heart weighs it down but a kind word makes it glad.

PROVERBS 12:25

By the fruit of his lips, a man enjoys good things; but the unfaithful crave violence.

PROVERBS 13:2

He who guards his mouth guards his soul. One who opens wide his lips comes to ruin.

PROVERBS 13:3

A righteous man hates lies but a wicked man brings shame and disgrace.

PROVERBS 13:5

The fool's talk brings a rod to his back but the lips of the wise protect them.

PROVERBS 14:3

A gentle answer turns away wrath but a harsh word stirs up anger.

PROVERBS 15:1

A gentle tongue is a tree of life but deceit in it crushes the spirit.

PROVERBS 15:4

Joy comes to a man with the reply of his mouth. How good is a word at the right time.

PROVERBS 15:23

The LORD detests the thoughts of the wicked but the thoughts of the pure are pleasing.

PROVERBS 15:26

The heart of the righteous weighs answers but the mouth of the wicked gushes out evil.

PROVERBS 15:28

The wise in heart shall be called prudent. Pleasantness of the lips promotes instruction.

PROVERBS 16:21

Pleasant words are a honeycomb, sweet to the soul and health to the bones.

PROVERBS 16:24

A worthless man devises mischief. His speech is like a scorching fire.

PROVERBS 16:27

The words of a man's mouth are like deep waters. The fountain of wisdom is like a flowing brook.

PROVERBS 18:4

A fool's mouth is his destruction and his lips are a snare to his soul.

PROVERBS 18:7

A man's stomach is filled with the fruit of his mouth. With the harvest of his lips he is satisfied. Death and life are in the power of the tongue; those who love it will eat its fruit.

PROVERBS 18:20-21

Whoever guards his mouth and his tongue keeps his soul from troubles.

PROVERBS 21:23

A word fitly spoken is like apples of gold in settings of silver.

PROVERBS 25:11

WEALTH

The prospect of the righteous is joy but the hope of the wicked will perish.

PROVERBS 11:28

There are some who pretend to be rich yet have nothing. There are some who pretend to be poor yet have great wealth.

PROVERBS 13:7

The ransom of a man's life is his riches but the poor hear no threats.

PROVERBS 13:8

Wealth gained dishonestly dwindles away but he who gathers by hand makes it grow.

PROVERBS 13:11

The crown of the wise is their riches but the folly of fools crowns them with folly.

PROVERBS 14:24

In the house of the righteous is much treasure but the income of the wicked brings trouble.

PROVERBS 15:6

Better is little, with the fear of the LORD, than great treasure with trouble.

PROVERBS 15:16

The name of the LORD is a strong tower; the righteous run into it and are safe. The rich man's wealth is his strong city, like an unscalable wall in his own imagination.

PROVERBS 18:10-11

Better is the poor who walks in his integrity than he who is perverse in his lips and is a fool.

PROVERBS 19:1

Wealth adds many friends but the poor is separated from his friend.

PROVERBS 19:4

He who gets wisdom loves his own soul. He who keeps understanding shall find good.

PROVERBS 19:8

An inheritance quickly gained at the beginning, won't be blessed in the end.

PROVERBS 20:21

He who loves pleasure shall be a poor man. He who loves wine and oil shall not be rich.

PROVERBS 21:17

There is precious treasure and oil in the dwelling of the wise; but a foolish man swallows it up.

PROVERBS 21:20

A good name is more desirable than great riches and loving favor is better than silver and gold.

PROVERBS 22:1

The result of humility and the fear of the LORD is wealth, honor and life.

PROVERBS 22:4

Do not weary yourself to be rich. In your wisdom, show restraint. Why do you set your eyes on that which is not? For it certainly sprouts wings like an eagle and flies in the sky.

PROVERBS 23:4-5

Know well the state of your flocks and pay attention to your herds: for riches are not forever, nor does even the crown endure to all generations. The hay is removed and the new growth appears, the grasses of the hills are gathered in. The lambs are for your clothing and the goats are the price of a field. There will be plenty of goats' milk for your food, for your family's food and for the nourishment of your servant girls.

PROVERBS 27:23-27

Better is the poor who walks in his integrity than he who is perverse in his ways and he is rich.

PROVERBS 28:6

He who increases his wealth by excessive interest gathers it for one who has pity on the poor.

PROVERBS 28:8

A faithful man is rich with blessings; but one who is eager to be rich will not go unpunished.

PROVERBS 28:20

A stingy man hurries after riches and doesn't know that poverty waits for him.

PROVERBS 28:22

HELPING OTHERS

He who has pity on the poor lends to the LORD; he will reward him.

PROVERBS 19:17

Whoever stops his ears at the cry of the poor, he will also cry out but shall not be heard.

PROVERBS 21:13

He who has a generous eye will be blessed; for he shares his food with the poor.

PROVERBS 22:9

Rescue those who are being led away to death. Indeed, hold back those who are staggering to the slaughter. If you say, "Look, we did not know this;" doesn't he who weighs the hearts consider it? He who keeps your soul, doesn't he know it? Shall he not render to every man according to his work?

PROVERBS 24:11-12

Do not forsake your friend and your father's friend. Do not go to your brother's house in the day of your disaster: better is a neighbor who is near than a distant brother.

PROVERBS 27:10

Open your mouth for the mute, in the cause of all who are left desolate. Open your mouth, judge righteously and serve justice to the poor and needy."

PROVERBS 31:8-9

FRIENDSHIP

One who walks with wise men grows wise but a companion of fools suffers harm.

PROVERBS 13:20

Stay away from a foolish man, for you won't find knowledge on his lips.

PROVERBS 14:7

When a man's ways please the LORD, he makes even his enemies to be at peace with him.

PROVERBS 16:7

A perverse man stirs up strife and a gossip separates close friends. A man of violence entices his neighbor and leads him in a way that is not good.

PROVERBS 16:28-29

He who covers an offense promotes love but he who repeats a matter separates best friends.

PROVERBS 17:9

A friend loves at all times and a brother is born for adversity.

PROVERBS 17:17

A man of many companions may be ruined but there is a friend who sticks closer than a brother.

PROVERBS 18:24

Wealth adds many friends but the poor is separated from his friend.

PROVERBS 19:4

All the relatives of the poor shun him: how much more do his friends avoid him. He pursues them with pleas but they are gone.

PROVERBS 19:7

He who goes about as a talebearer reveals secrets; therefore do not keep company with him who opens wide his lips.

PROVERBS 20:19

He who loves purity of heart and speaks gracefully is the king's friend.

PROVERBS 22:11

Do not befriend a hot-tempered man and do not associate with one who harbors anger: lest you learn his ways and ensnare your soul.

PROVERBS 22:24-25

Listen, my son, and be wise, and keep your heart on the right path. Do not be among ones drinking too much wine or those who gorge themselves on meat.

PROVERBS 23:19-20

An honest answer is like a kiss on the lips.

PROVERBS 24:26

Faithful are the wounds of a friend; although the kisses of an enemy are profuse.

PROVERBS 27:6

Do not forsake your friend and your father's friend. Do not go to your brother's house in the day of your disaster: better is a neighbor who is near than a distant brother.

PROVERBS 27:10

He who blesses his neighbor with a loud voice early in the morning, it will be taken as a curse by him.

PROVERBS 27:14

Whoever keeps the Law is a wise son but he who is a companion of gluttons shames his father.

PROVERBS 28:7

A man who flatters his neighbor spreads a net for his feet.

PROVERBS 29:5

PARENT AND CHILD RELATIONSHIP

My son, listen to your father's instruction and do not forsake your mother's teaching: for they will be a garland to grace your head and a necklace around your neck.

PROVERBS 1:8-9

Listen, sons, to a father's instruction. Pay attention and know understanding.

PROVERBS 4:1

My son, keep your father's commandment and do not forsake your mother's teaching. Bind them continually on your heart. Tie them around your neck. When you walk, it will lead you. When you sleep, it will watch over you. When you awake, it will talk with you. For the commandment is a lamp and the Law is light. Reproofs of instruction are the way of life, to keep you from the immoral woman, from the flattery of the foreign woman.

PROVERBS 6:20-24

A wise son makes a glad father but a foolish son brings grief to his mother.

PROVERBS 10:1

A wise son listens to his father's instruction but a scoffer doesn't listen to rebuke.

PROVERBS 13:1

One who spares the rod hates his son but one who loves him is careful to discipline him.

PROVERBS 13:24

A fool despises his father's correction but he who heeds reproof shows prudence.

PROVERBS 15:5

A wise son makes a father glad but a foolish man despises his mother.

PROVERBS 15:20

Whoever rewards evil for good, evil shall not depart from his house.

PROVERBS 17:13

He who becomes the father of a fool grieves. The father of a fool has no joy.

PROVERBS 17:21

A foolish son brings grief to his father and bitterness to her who bore him.

PROVERBS 17:25

A foolish son is the calamity of his father. A wife's quarrels are a continual dripping.

PROVERBS 19:13

Discipline your son, for there is hope; do not be a willing party to his death.

PROVERBS 19:18

He who robs his father and drives away his mother is a son who causes shame and brings reproach.

A righteous man walks in integrity; blessed are his children after him.

PROVERBS 20:7

Whoever curses his father or his mother, his lamp shall be put out in blackness of darkness.

PROVERBS 20:20

Train a child in the way he should go and when he is old he will not depart from it.

PROVERBS 22:6

Folly is bound up in the heart of a child: the rod of discipline drives it far from him.

PROVERBS 22:15

Do not withhold correction from a child. If you punish him with the rod, he will not die. Punish him with the rod and save his soul from Sheol.

PROVERBS 23:13-14

Listen to your father who gave you life and do not despise your mother when she is old.

PROVERBS 23:22

The father of the righteous has great joy. Whoever fathers a wise child delights in him. Let your father and your mother be glad. Let her who bore you rejoice.

PROVERBS 23:24-25

Whoever robs his father or his mother and says, "It's not wrong." He is a partner with a destroyer.

PROVERBS 28:24

Whoever loves wisdom brings joy to his father but a companion of prostitutes squanders his wealth.

PROVERBS 29:3

The rod of correction gives wisdom but a child left to himself causes shame to his mother.

PROVERBS 29:15

Correct your son and he will give you peace; yes, he will bring delight to your soul.

PROVERBS 29:17

The eye that mocks at his father and scorns obedience to his mother: the ravens of the valley shall pick it out, the young eagles shall eat it.

PROVERBS 30:17

ANGER

He who is slow to anger has great understanding but he who has a quick temper displays folly.

PROVERBS 14:29

A gentle answer turns away wrath but a harsh word stirs up anger.

PROVERBS 15:1

Better is a dinner of herbs, where love is, than a fattened calf with hatred.

PROVERBS 15:17

A wrathful man stirs up contention but one who is slow to anger appeases strife.

PROVERBS 15:18

The king's wrath is a messenger of death but a wise man will pacify it.

PROVERBS 16:14

The discretion of a man makes him slow to anger. It is his glory to overlook an offense.

PROVERBS 19:11

The king's wrath is like the roaring of a lion but his favor is like dew on the grass.

PROVERBS 19:12

A hot-tempered man must pay the penalty, for if you rescue him, you must do it again.

PROVERBS 19:19

The terror of a king is like the roaring of a lion. He who provokes him to anger forfeits his own life.

PROVERBS 20:2

A gift in secret pacifies anger; and a bribe in the cloak, strong wrath.

PROVERBS 21:14

Like a city that is broken down and without walls is a man whose spirit is without restraint.

PROVERBS 25:28

A fool vents all of his anger but a wise man brings himself under control.

PROVERBS 29:11

An angry man stirs up strife and a wrathful man abounds in sin.

PROVERBS 29:22

For as the churning of milk brings forth butter and the wringing of the nose brings forth blood; so the forcing of wrath brings forth strife.

PROVERBS 30:33

ARGUMENTS

Like one who grabs a dog's ears is one who passes by and meddles in a quarrel not his own.

PROVERBS 26:17

Without wood a fire goes out. Without gossip, contention ceases.

PROVERBS 26:20

An angry man stirs up strife and a wrathful man abounds in sin.

PROVERBS 29:22

LAZINESS AND PASSIVITY

Go to the ant, you sluggard. Consider her ways and be wise; which having no chief, overseer, or ruler, provides her bread in the summer and gathers her food in the harvest.

PROVERBS 6:6-8

How long will you sleep, sluggard? When will you arise out of your sleep? A little sleep, a little slumber, a little folding of the hands to sleep: so your poverty will come as a robber and your scarcity as an armed man.

PROVERBS 6:9-11

He becomes poor who works with a lazy hand but the hand of the diligent brings wealth.

PROVERBS 10:4

He who gathers in summer is a wise son but he who sleeps during the harvest is a son who causes shame.

PROVERBS 10:5

As vinegar to the teeth and as smoke to the eyes so is the sluggard to those who send him.

PROVERBS 10:26

A gracious woman obtains honor but she who hates virtue makes a throne for dishonor. The slothful become destitute and ruthless men grab wealth.

PROVERBS 11:16

Better is he who is lightly esteemed and has a servant than he who honors himself and lacks bread.

PROVERBS 12:9

He who tills his land shall have plenty of bread but he who chases fantasies is void of understanding.

PROVERBS 12:11

The hands of the diligent ones shall rule but laziness ends in slave labor.

PROVERBS 12:24

The slothful man doesn't roast his game but the possessions of diligent men are prized.

PROVERBS 12:27

The soul of the sluggard desires and has nothing but the desire of the diligent shall be fully satisfied.

PROVERBS 13:4

Wealth gained dishonestly dwindles away but he who gathers by hand makes it grow.

PROVERBS 13:11

In all hard work there is profit but the talk of the lips leads only to poverty.

PROVERBS 14:23

The way of the sluggard is like a thorn patch but the path of the upright is a highway.

PROVERBS 15:19

The appetite of the laboring man labors for him, for his mouth urges him on.

PROVERBS 16:26

One who is slack in his work is brother to him who is a master of destruction.

PROVERBS 18:9

Slothfulness casts into a deep sleep. The idle soul shall suffer hunger.

PROVERBS 19:15

The sluggard buries his hand in the dish, he will not so much as bring it to his mouth again.

PROVERBS 19:24

The sluggard will not plow by reason of the winter, therefore he shall beg in harvest and have nothing.

PROVERBS 20:4

Do not love sleep, lest you come to poverty. Open your eyes, and you shall be satisfied with bread.

PROVERBS 20:13

An inheritance quickly gained at the beginning, won't be blessed in the end.

PROVERBS 20:21

The desire of the sluggard kills him, for his hands refuse to labor. There are those who covet greedily all day long; but the righteous give and do not withhold.

PROVERBS 21:25-26

The sluggard says, "There is a lion outside. I will be killed in the streets."

PROVERBS 22:13

Do you see a man skilled in his work? He will serve kings. He won't serve obscure men.

PROVERBS 22:29

The drunkard and the glutton shall become poor; and drowsiness clothes them in rags.

PROVERBS 23:21

I went by the field of the sluggard, by the vineyard of the man void of understanding; look, it was all grown over with thorns. Its surface was covered with nettles and its stone wall was broken down. Then I saw and considered well. I saw and received instruction: a little sleep, a little slumber, a little folding of the hands to sleep; so your poverty will come as a robber and your want as an armed man.

PROVERBS 24:30-34

The sluggard says, "There is a lion in the road. A fierce lion roams the streets." As the door turns on its hinges, so does the sluggard on his bed. The sluggard buries his hand in the dish. He is too lazy to bring it back to his mouth. The sluggard is wiser in his own eyes than seven men who answer with discretion.

PROVERBS 26:13-16

One who works his land will have an abundance of food; but one who chases fantasies will have his fill of poverty.

PROVERBS 28:19

TAKE CARE OF YOUR WELLBEING

Do not be wise in your own eyes. Fear the LORD and depart from evil. It will be health to your body and nourishment to your bones.

PROVERBS 3:7-8

Length of days is in her (wisdom's) right hand. In her left hand are riches and honor. Her ways are ways of pleasantness. All her paths are peace. She is a tree of life to those who lay hold of her and those who hold on to her are blessed.

PROVERBS 3:16-18

My son, let them not depart from your eyes. Keep sound wisdom and discretion: so they will be life to your soul and grace for your neck.

PROVERBS 3:21-22

Listen, my son, and receive my sayings. The years of your life will be many.

PROVERBS 4:10

My son, attend to my words. Turn your ear to my sayings. Let them not depart from your eyes. Keep them in the midst of your heart. For they are life to him who finds them and health to all of his body.

PROVERBS 4:20-22

For by me your days will be multiplied. The years of your life will be increased. If you are wise, you are wise for yourself. If you mock, you alone will bear it.

PROVERBS 9:11-12

The fear of the LORD prolongs days but the years of the wicked shall be shortened.

PROVERBS 10:27

The life of the body is a heart at peace but envy rots the bones.

PROVERBS 14:30

Pleasant words are a honeycomb, sweet to the soul and health to the bones.

PROVERBS 16:24

Gray hair is a crown of glory. It is found in the path of righteousness.

PROVERBS 16:31

Better is a dry morsel with quietness than a house full of feasting with strife.

PROVERBS 17:1

A cheerful heart makes good medicine but a crushed spirit dries up the bones.

PROVERBS 17:22

A man's spirit will sustain him in sickness but a crushed spirit, who can bear?

PROVERBS 18:14

He who keeps the commandment keeps his soul but he who is contemptuous in his ways shall die.

PROVERBS 19:16

The fear of the LORD leads to life, then contentment; he rests and will not be touched by trouble.

PROVERBS 19:23

Getting treasures by a lying tongue is a fleeting vapor for those who seek death.

PROVERBS 21:6

The man who wanders out of the way of understanding shall rest in the assembly of the dead.

PROVERBS 21:16

He who follows after righteousness and kindness finds life, righteousness and honor.

PROVERBS 21:21

Thorns and snares are in the path of the wicked: whoever guards his soul stays from them.

PROVERBS 22:5

Perfume and incense bring joy to the heart; so does earnest counsel from a man's friend.

PROVERBS 27:9

A faithful man is rich with blessings but one who is eager to be rich will not go unpunished.

PROVERBS 28:20

ADVICE TO YOUNG MEN

The fear of the LORD is the beginning of knowledge but the foolish despise wisdom and instruction. My son, listen to your father's instruction and do not forsake your mother's teaching: for they will be a garland to grace your head and a necklace around your neck.

My son, if sinners entice you, do not consent. If they say, "Come with us, let's lie in wait for blood; let's lurk secretly for the innocent without cause; let's swallow them up alive like Sheol, and whole, like those who go down into the pit. We'll find all valuable wealth. We'll fill our houses with spoil. Throw in your lot with us. We'll all have one purse."

My son, do not walk in the way with them. Keep your foot from their path, for their feet run to evil. They hurry to shed blood. For in vain is the net spread in the sight of any bird: but these lie in wait for their own blood. They lurk secretly for their own lives. So are the ways of everyone who is greedy for gain. It takes away the life of its owners.

PROVERBS 1:7-19

My son, do not forget my teaching; but let your heart keep my commandments: for length of days, and years of life, and peace, will they add to you. Do not let kindness and truth forsake you. Bind them around your neck. Write them on the tablet of your heart. So you will find favor and good understanding in the sight of God and man.

Trust in the LORD with all your heart and do not lean on your own understanding. In all your ways acknowledge him and he will make your paths straight. Do not be wise in your own eyes. Fear the LORD and depart from evil. It will be health to your body and nourishment to your bones.

Honor the LORD with your substance, with the first fruits of all your increase: so your storehouses will be filled with plenty and your vats will overflow with new wine. My son, do not despise the discipline of the LORD, nor resent his correction. For whom the LORD loves he disciplines and punishes every son he accepts. Blessed is the man who finds wisdom, the man who gets understanding. For her good profit is better than getting silver and her return is better than fine gold. She is more precious than rubies. None of the things you can desire are to be compared to her. Length of days is in her right hand. In her left hand are riches and honor. Her ways are ways of pleasantness. All her paths are peace. She is a tree of life to those who lay hold of her and those who hold on to her are blessed.

By wisdom the LORD founded the earth. By understanding, he established the heavens. By his knowledge, the depths were broken up and the skies drop down the dew. My son, let them not depart from your eyes. Keep sound wisdom and discretion: so they will be life to your soul and grace for your neck.

Then you shall walk in your way securely and your foot won't stumble. When you lie down, you will not be afraid; you will lie down and your sleep will be sweet. Do not be afraid of sudden fear or of the storm of the wicked when it comes: for the LORD will be your confidence and will keep your foot from being taken. Do not withhold good from those to whom it is due, when it is in the power of your hand to do it.

Do not say to your neighbor, "Go and come again; tomorrow I will give it to you," when you have it by you. Do not devise evil against your neighbor, seeing he dwells securely by you. Do not strive with a man without cause, if he has done you no harm. Do not envy the man of violence. Choose none of his ways. For the perverse is an abomination to the LORD but his friendship is with the upright. The LORD's curse is in the house of the wicked but he blesses the habitation of the righteous. Surely he is scornful to scoffers but he gives grace to the humble. The wise will inherit glory but shame will be the promotion of fools.

PROVERBS 3:1-35

THE CAPABLE WIFE

A worthy woman is the crown of her husband but a disgraceful wife is as rottenness in his bones.

PROVERBS 12:4

Every wise woman builds her house but the foolish one tears it down with her own hands.

PROVERBS 14:1

Whoever finds a wife finds a good thing and obtains favor of the LORD.

PROVERBS 18:22

House and riches are an inheritance from fathers but a prudent wife is from the LORD.

PROVERBS 19:14

It is better to dwell in the corner of the housetop than to share a house with a contentious woman.

PROVERBS 21:9

It is better to dwell in a desert land than with a contentious and fretful woman.

PROVERBS 21:19

A continual dropping on a rainy day and a contentious wife are alike: restraining her is like restraining the wind or like grasping oil in his right hand.

PROVERBS 27:15-16

Who can find a worthy woman? For her price is far above rubies.

The heart of her husband trusts in her. He shall have no lack of gain.

She does him good and not harm, all the days of her life.

She seeks wool and flax and works eagerly with her hands.

She is like the merchant ships. She brings her bread from afar.

She rises also while it is yet night, gives food to her household and portions for her servant girls.

She considers a field and buys it. With the fruit of her hands, she plants a vineyard.

She girds her waist with strength and makes her arms strong.

She perceives that her merchandise is profitable. Her lamp doesn't go out by night.

She lays her hands to the distaff and her hands hold the spindle.

She opens her arms to the poor; yes, she extends her hands to the needy.

She is not afraid of the snow for her household; for all her household are clothed with scarlet.

She makes for herself carpets of tapestry. Her clothing is fine linen and purple.

Her husband is respected in the gates, when he sits among the elders of the land.

She makes linen garments and sells them and delivers sashes to the merchant.

Strength and dignity are her clothing. She laughs at the time to come.

She opens her mouth with wisdom. Faithful instruction is on her tongue.

She looks well to the ways of her household and doesn't eat the bread of idleness.
Her children rise up and call her blessed. Her husband also praises her:
"Many women do noble things but you excel them all."
Charm is deceitful and beauty is vain; but a woman who fears the LORD, she shall be praised.
Give her of the fruit of her hands. Let her works praise her in the gates.

PROVERBS 31:10-31

DRINKING

Wine is a mocker and beer is a brawler. Whoever is led astray by them is not wise.

PROVERBS 20:1

Listen, my son, and be wise, and keep your heart on the right path. Do not be among ones drinking too much wine or those who gorge themselves on meat: for the drunkard and the glutton shall become poor; and drowsiness clothes them in rags.

PROVERBS 23:19-21

Who has woe? Who has sorrow? Who has strife? Who has complaints? Who has needless bruises? Who has bloodshot eyes? Those who stay long at the wine; those who go to seek out mixed wine. Do not look at the wine when it is red, when it sparkles in the cup, when it goes down smoothly. In the end, it bites like a serpent, and poisons like a viper. Your eyes will see strange things and your mind will imagine confusing things. Yes, you will be as he who lies down in the midst of the sea or as he who lies on top of the rigging: "They hit me and I was not hurt. They beat me and I do not feel it. When will I wake up? I can do it again. I can find another."

PROVERBS 23:29-35

It is not for kings, O Lemuel; it is not for kings to drink wine or for princes to take strong drink, lest they drink, and forget the decree and pervert the justice due to anyone who is afflicted.

Give strong drink to him who is ready to perish; and wine to the bitter in soul: Let him drink, and forget his poverty and remember his misery no more.

PROVERBS 31:4-7

ENEMY

When a man's ways please the LORD, he makes even his enemies to be at peace with him.

PROVERBS 16:7

Do not rejoice when your enemy falls. Do not let your heart be glad when he is overthrown; lest the LORD see it, and it displease him and he turn away his wrath from him.

PROVERBS 24:17-18

If your enemy is hungry, give him something to eat. If he is thirsty, give him something to drink, for you will heap coals of fire on his head and the LORD will reward you.

PROVERBS 25:21-22

Faithful are the wounds of a friend; although the kisses of an enemy are profuse.

PROVERBS 27:6

Whoever is an accomplice of a thief is an enemy of his own soul. He takes an oath but dares not testify.

PROVERBS 29:24

SELF CONTROL

The evil deeds of the wicked ensnare him. The cords of his sin hold him firmly. He will die for lack of instruction. In the greatness of his folly, he will go astray.

PROVERBS 5:22-23

In the multitude of words there is no lack of disobedience, but he who restrains his lips does wisely.

PROVERBS 10:19

A fool shows his annoyance the same day but one who overlooks an insult is prudent.

PROVERBS 12:16

A prudent man keeps his knowledge but the hearts of fools proclaim foolishness.

PROVERBS 12:23

He who is quick to become angry will commit folly and a crafty man is hated.

PROVERBS 14:17

He who is slow to anger has great understanding but he who has a quick temper displays folly.

PROVERBS 14:29

A wrathful man stirs up contention but one who is slow to anger appeases strife.

PROVERBS 15:18

One who is slow to anger is better than the mighty; one who rules his spirit, than he who takes a city.

PROVERBS 16:32

He who spares his words has knowledge. He who is even tempered is a man of understanding.

PROVERBS 17:27

It isn't good to have zeal without knowledge; nor being hasty with one's feet and missing the way.

PROVERBS 19:2

The discretion of a man makes him slow to anger. It is his glory to overlook an offense.

PROVERBS 19:11

Like a city that is broken down and without walls is a man whose spirit is without restraint.

PROVERBS 25:28

A fool vents all of his anger but a wise man brings himself under control.

PROVERBS 29:11

INSECURITY

But whoever listens to me will dwell securely and will be at ease, without fear of harm."

PROVERBS 1:33

He (the Lord) lays up sound wisdom for the upright. He is a shield to those who walk in integrity; that he may guard the paths of justice and preserve the way of his faithful ones.

PROVERBS 2:7-8

My son, let them not depart from your eyes. Keep sound wisdom and discretion: so they will be life to your soul and grace for your neck. Then you shall walk in your way securely and your foot won't stumble. When you lie down, you will not be afraid; you will lie down and your sleep will be sweet. Do not be afraid of sudden fear or of the storm of the wicked when it comes: for the LORD will be your confidence and will keep your foot from being taken.

PROVERBS 3:21-26

Do not forsake her (wisdom) and she will preserve you. Love her and she will keep you.

PROVERBS 4:6

He who walks blamelessly walks surely but he who perverts his ways will be found out.

PROVERBS 10:9

The way of the LORD is a stronghold to the upright, but it is a destruction to evildoers. The righteous will never be removed but the wicked will not dwell in the land.

PROVERBS 10:29-30

Where there is no wise guidance, the nation falls, but in the multitude of counselors there is victory.

PROVERBS 11:14

A man shall not be established by wickedness but the root of the righteous shall not be moved.

PROVERBS 12:3

In the fear of the LORD is a secure fortress and he will be a refuge for his children.

PROVERBS 14:26

The name of the LORD is a strong tower; the righteous run into it and are safe. The rich man's wealth is his strong city, like an unscalable wall in his own imagination.

PROVERBS 18:10-11

The fear of man proves to be a snare but whoever puts his trust in the LORD will be set on high.

PROVERBS 29:25

HAPPINESS

He who despises his neighbor sins but blessed is he who shows kindness to the poor.

PROVERBS 14:21

The father of the righteous has great joy. Whoever fathers a wise child delights in him.

PROVERBS 23:24

Let your father and your mother be glad. Let her who bore you rejoice.

PROVERBS 23:25

Blessed is the man who is always reverent but the one who hardens his heart will fall into evil.

PROVERBS 28:14

An evil man is snared by his sin but the righteous can sing and be glad.

PROVERBS 29:6

WARNING AGAINST ADULTERY

My son, if you will receive my words and store up my commandments within you; then you will understand righteousness and justice, equity and every good path. For wisdom will enter into your heart. Knowledge will be pleasant to your soul. To deliver you from the strange woman, even from the foreigner who flatters with her words; who forsakes the friend of her youth and forgets the covenant of her God: for her house leads down to death, her paths to the dead. None who go to her return again, neither do they attain to the paths of life.

PROVERBS 2:1, 9-10, 16-19

My son, pay attention to my wisdom. Turn your ear to my understanding: that you may maintain discretion, that your lips may preserve knowledge. For the lips of an adulteress drip honey. Her mouth is smoother than oil but in the end she is as bitter as wormwood and as sharp as a two-edged sword. Her feet go down to death. Her steps lead straight to Sheol. She gives no thought to the way of life. Her ways are crooked and she doesn't know it.

Now therefore, son, listen to me. Do not depart from the words of my mouth. Remove your way far from her. Do not come near the door of her house, lest you give your honor to others and your years to the merciless; lest strangers feast on your wealth and your labors enrich another man's house.

You will groan at your latter end, when your flesh and your body are consumed and say, "How I have hated instruction, and my heart despised reproof; neither have I obeyed the voice of my teachers, nor turned my ear to those who instructed me. I have come to the brink of utter ruin, in the midst of the gathered assembly."

Drink water out of your own cistern, running water out of your own well. Should your springs overflow in the streets, streams of water in the public squares? Let them be for yourself alone, not for strangers with you. Let your spring be blessed. Rejoice in the wife of your youth. A loving doe and a graceful deer — let her breasts satisfy you at all times. Be captivated always with her love. For why should you, my son, be captivated with an adulteress? Why embrace the bosom of another?

For the ways of man are before the eyes of the LORD. He examines all his paths. The evil deeds of the wicked ensnare him. The cords of his sin hold him firmly. He will die for lack of instruction. In the greatness of his folly, he will go astray.

PROVERBS 5:1-23

My son, keep your father's commandment and do not forsake your mother's teaching. Bind them continually on your heart. Tie them around your neck. When you walk, it will lead you. When you sleep, it will watch over you. When you awake, it will talk with you. For the commandment is a lamp and the Law is light. Reproofs of instruction are the way of life, to keep you from the immoral woman, from the flattery of the foreign woman. Do not lust after her beauty in your heart, neither let her captivate you with her eyelids. For a prostitute reduces you to a piece of bread.

The adulteress hunts for your precious life.

Can a man scoop fire into his lap and his clothes not be burned? Or can one walk on hot coals and his feet not be scorched? So is he who goes in to his neighbor's wife. Whoever touches her will not be unpunished. Men do not despise a thief, if he steals to satisfy himself when he is hungry: but if he is found, he must repay seven times. He shall give all the wealth of his house. He who commits adultery with a woman is void of understanding. He who does it destroys his own soul. He will get wounds and dishonor. His reproach will not be wiped away. For jealousy arouses the fury of the husband. He won't spare in the day of vengeance. He won't regard any ransom, neither will he rest content, though you give many gifts.

PROVERBS 6:20-35

My son, keep my words. Lay up my commandments within you. Keep my commandments and live. Guard my teaching as the apple of your eye. Bind them on your fingers. Write them on the tablet of your heart. Tell wisdom, "You are my sister." Call understanding your relative, that they may keep you from the strange woman, from the foreigner who flatters with her words.

For at the window of my house, I looked out through my lattice. I saw among the simple ones. I discerned among the youths a young man void of understanding, passing through the street near her corner, he went the way to her house, in the twilight, in the evening of the day, in the middle of the night and in the darkness. Look, there a woman met him with the attire of a prostitute and with crafty intent.

She is loud and defiant. Her feet do not stay in her house. Now she is in the streets, now in the squares and lurking at every corner. So she caught him and kissed him. With an impudent face she said to him: "Sacrifices of peace offerings are with me. This day I have paid my vows. Therefore I came out to meet you, to diligently seek your face and I have found you. I have spread my couch with carpets of tapestry, with striped cloths of the yarn of Egypt. I have perfumed my bed with myrrh, aloes and cinnamon. Come, let's take our fill of loving until the morning. Let's solace ourselves with loving.

For my husband isn't at home. He has gone on a long journey. He has taken a bag of money with him. He will come home at the full moon." With persuasive words, she led him astray. With the flattering of her lips, she seduced him. He followed her immediately, as an ox goes to the slaughter, as a fool to the correction of the stocks.
Until an arrow strikes through his liver, as a bird hurries to the snare and doesn't know that it will cost his life. Now therefore, son, listen to me. Pay attention to the words of my mouth. Do not let your heart turn to her ways. Do not go astray in her path, for she has thrown down many wounded. Yes, all her slain are a mighty army.
Her house is the way to Sheol, going down to the chambers of death.

PROVERBS 7:1-27

The mouth of an adulteress is a deep pit: he who is under the LORD's wrath will fall into it.

PROVERBS 22:14

For a prostitute is a deep pit and a wayward wife is a narrow well. Yes, she lies in wait like a robber and increases the unfaithful among men.

PROVERBS 23:27-28

Whoever loves wisdom brings joy to his father but a companion of prostitutes squanders his wealth.

PROVERBS 29:3

So is the way of an adulterous woman: she eats and wipes her mouth and says, 'I have done nothing wrong.'

PROVERBS 30:20

JUSTICE

To be partial to the faces of the wicked is not good nor to deprive the innocent of justice.

PROVERBS 18:5

A corrupt witness mocks justice and the mouth of the wicked gulps down iniquity.

PROVERBS 19:28

It is joy to the righteous to do justice but it is a destruction to evildoers.

PROVERBS 21:15

He who sows wickedness reaps trouble and the rod of his fury will be destroyed.

PROVERBS 22:8

These also are sayings of the wise. To show partiality in judgment is not good. He who says to the wicked, "You are righteous;" peoples shall curse him and nations shall abhor him but it will go well with those who convict the guilty and a rich blessing will come on them.

PROVERBS 24:23-25

Evil men do not understand justice but those who seek the LORD understand it fully.

PROVERBS 28:5

The king by justice makes the land stable but he who takes bribes tears it down.

PROVERBS 29:4

Many seek the ruler's favor but a man's justice comes from the LORD.

PROVERBS 29:26

HUMILITY AND PRIDE

The LORD's curse is in the house of the wicked but he blesses the habitation of the righteous. Surely he is scornful to scoffers but he gives grace to the humble.

PROVERBS 3:33-34

When pride comes then comes shame but with humility comes wisdom.

PROVERBS 11:2

Pride only breeds quarrels but with ones who take advice is wisdom.

PROVERBS 13:10

The fool's talk brings a rod to his back but the lips of the wise protect them.

PROVERBS 14:3

A scoffer seeks wisdom and doesn't find it but knowledge comes easily to a discerning person.

PROVERBS 14:6

The evil bow down before the good and the wicked at the gates of the righteous.

PROVERBS 14:19

A scoffer doesn't love to be reproved; he will not go to the wise.

PROVERBS 15:12

The LORD will uproot the house of the proud but he will keep the widow's borders intact.

PROVERBS 15:25

The fear of the LORD teaches wisdom. Before honor is humility.

PROVERBS 15:33

Everyone who is proud in heart is an abomination to the LORD: they shall certainly not be unpunished.

PROVERBS 16:5

Pride goes before destruction and a haughty spirit before a fall. It is better to be of a lowly spirit with the poor than to divide the plunder with the proud.

PROVERBS 16:18-19

Children's children are the crown of old men; the glory of children are their parents.

PROVERBS 17:6

Before destruction the heart of man is proud but before honor is humility.

PROVERBS 18:12

Flog a scoffer and the simple will learn prudence; rebuke one who has understanding and he will gain knowledge.

PROVERBS 19:25

The proud and haughty man, "scoffer" is his name; he works in the arrogance of pride.

PROVERBS 21:24

The result of humility and the fear of the LORD is wealth, honor and life.

PROVERBS 22:4

A man's pride brings him low but one of lowly spirit gains honor.

PROVERBS 29:23

If you have done foolishly in lifting up yourself or if you have thought evil, put your hand over your mouth.

PROVERBS 30:32

TEMPTATION

My son, if sinners entice you, do not consent.... My son, do not walk in the way with them. Keep your foot from their path.

PROVERBS 1:10, 15

Do not enter into the path of the wicked. Do not walk in the way of evil men. Avoid it and do not pass by it. Turn from it and pass on. For they do not sleep, unless they do evil. Their sleep is taken away, unless they make someone fall. For they eat the bread of wickedness and drink the wine of violence.

PROVERBS 4:14-17

Do not turn to the right hand nor to the left. Remove your foot from evil.

PROVERBS 4:27

DILIGENCE

Guard your heart with all diligence, for out of it is the wellspring of life.

PROVERBS 4:23

I (the Lord) love those who love me. Those who seek me diligently will find me.

PROVERBS 8:17

He becomes poor who works with a lazy hand but the hand of the diligent brings wealth.

PROVERBS 10:4

The hands of the diligent ones shall rule but laziness ends in slave labor.

PROVERBS 12:24

The soul of the sluggard desires and has nothing but the desire of the diligent shall be fully satisfied.

PROVERBS 13:4

The plans of the diligent surely lead to profit and everyone who is hasty surely rushes to poverty.

PROVERBS 21:5

FAVOUR

Do not let kindness and truth forsake you. Bind them around your neck. Write them on the tablet of your heart. So you will find favor and good understanding in the sight of God and man.

PROVERBS 3:3-4

Surely he is scornful to scoffers but he gives grace to the humble.

PROVERBS 3:34

The merciful man does good to his own soul but he who is cruel troubles his own flesh.

PROVERBS 11:17

He who diligently seeks good seeks favor but he who searches after evil, it shall come to him.

PROVERBS 11:27

A good man shall obtain favor from the LORD but he will condemn a man of wicked devices.

PROVERBS 12:2

Fools mock at making atonement for sins but among the upright there is good will.

PROVERBS 14:9

The evil bow down before the good and the wicked at the gates of the righteous.

PROVERBS 14:19

In the light of the king's face is life. His favor is like a cloud of the spring rain.

PROVERBS 16:15

To be partial to the faces of the wicked is not good nor to deprive the innocent of justice.

PROVERBS 18:5

Many will seek the favor of a ruler and everyone is a friend to a man who gives gifts.

PROVERBS 19:6

He who gets wisdom loves his own soul. He who keeps understanding shall find good.

PROVERBS 19:8

The king's wrath is like the roaring of a lion but his favor is like dew on the grass.

PROVERBS 19:12

ADVICE TO A KING

The words of king Lemuel; the oracle which his mother taught him.

"Oh, my son. Oh, son of my womb. Oh, son of my vows. Do not give your strength to women, nor your ways to that which destroys kings. It is not for kings, O Lemuel; it is not for kings to drink wine, for princes to take strong drink, lest they drink and forget the decree and pervert the justice due to anyone who is afflicted.

Give strong drink to him who is ready to perish; and wine to the bitter in soul: Let him drink, and forget his poverty, and remember his misery no more. Open your mouth for the mute, in the cause of all who are left desolate. Open your mouth, judge righteously and serve justice to the poor and needy."

PROVERBS 31:1-9

HONESTY

Treasures of wickedness profit nothing but righteousness delivers from death.

PROVERBS 10:2

He who walks blamelessly walks surely but he who perverts his ways will be found out.

PROVERBS 10:9

He who walks in his uprightness fears the LORD but he who is perverse in his ways despises him.

PROVERBS 14:2

The way of the sluggard is like a thorn patch but the path of the upright is a highway.

PROVERBS 15:19

He who is greedy for gain troubles his own house but he who hates bribes will live.

PROVERBS 15:27

By mercy and truth iniquity is atoned for. By the fear of the LORD men depart from evil.

PROVERBS 16:6

Better is a little with righteousness than great revenues with injustice.

PROVERBS 16:8

Honest balances and scales are the LORD's; all the weights in the bag are his work.

PROVERBS 16:11

Better is the poor who walks in his integrity than he who is perverse in his lips and is a fool.

PROVERBS 19:1

Even a child makes himself known by his doings, whether his work is pure and whether it is right.

PROVERBS 20:11

Fraudulent food is sweet to a man but afterwards his mouth is filled with gravel.

PROVERBS 20:17

The LORD detests differing weights and dishonest scales are not pleasing.

PROVERBS 20:23

Love and faithfulness keep the king safe. His throne is sustained by love.

PROVERBS 20:28

Getting treasures by a lying tongue is a fleeting vapor for those who seek death.

PROVERBS 21:6

He who follows after righteousness and kindness finds life, righteousness and honor.

PROVERBS 21:21

Do not lie in wait, wicked man, against the habitation of the righteous. Do not destroy his resting place: for a righteous man falls seven times and rises up again; but the wicked are overthrown by calamity.

PROVERBS 24:15-16

The wicked flee when no one pursues but the righteous are as bold as a lion.

PROVERBS 28:1

Better is the poor who walks in his integrity than he who is perverse in his ways and he is rich.

PROVERBS 28:6

Whoever causes the upright to go astray in an evil way, he will fall into his own trap but the blameless will inherit good.

PROVERBS 28:10

A prince who lacks understanding is a cruel oppressor but one who hates ill-gotten gain will prolong his days.

PROVERBS 28:16

Whoever walks blamelessly is kept safe but one with perverse ways will fall suddenly.

PROVERBS 28:18

A faithful man is rich with blessings but one who is eager to be rich will not go unpunished.

PROVERBS 28:20

An evil man is snared by his sin but the righteous can sing and be glad.

PROVERBS 29:6

The bloodthirsty hate a man of integrity and they seek the life of the upright.

PROVERBS 29:10

TRUTHFULNESS

Put away from yourself a perverse mouth. Put corrupt lips far from you.

PROVERBS 4:24

One winking with the eye causes sorrow but a chattering fool will fall.

PROVERBS 10:10

Righteous lips are the delight of kings. They value one who speaks the truth.

PROVERBS 16:13

Arrogant speech isn't fitting for a fool, much less do lying lips fit a prince.

PROVERBS 17:7

The eyes of the LORD watch over knowledge but he frustrates the words of the unfaithful.

PROVERBS 22:12

ENVY

Do not let your heart envy sinners but rather fear the LORD all the day long. For surely there is a future and your hope will not be cut off.

PROVERBS 23:17-18

Do not be envious of evil men; neither desire to be with them: for their hearts plot violence and their lips talk about mischief.

PROVERBS 24:1-2

Do not fret yourself because of evildoers; neither be envious of the wicked: for there will be no reward to the evil man and the lamp of the wicked shall be snuffed out.

PROVERBS 24:19-20

Wrath is cruel and anger is overwhelming but who is able to stand before jealousy?

PROVERBS 27:4

PLANNING

The plans of the diligent surely lead to profit and everyone who is hasty surely rushes to poverty.

PROVERBS 21:5

A wise man has great power and a knowledgeable man increases strength for by wise guidance you wage your war and victory is in many advisors.

PROVERBS 24:5-6

One who plots to do evil will be called a schemer. The schemes of folly are sin. The mocker is detested by men.

PROVERBS 24:8-9

SIN

Misfortune pursues sinners but prosperity rewards the righteous.

PROVERBS 13:21

A good man leaves an inheritance to his children's children but the wealth of the sinner is stored for the righteous.

PROVERBS 13:22

In rebellion, a land has many rulers, but order is maintained by a man of understanding and knowledge.

PROVERBS 28:2

He who conceals his sins doesn't prosper but whoever confesses and renounces them finds mercy.

PROVERBS 28:13

An evil man is snared by his sin but the righteous can sing and be glad.

PROVERBS 29:6

TALKING

There is gold and abundance of rubies but the lips of knowledge are a rare jewel.

PROVERBS 20:15

Whoever guards his mouth and his tongue keeps his soul from troubles.

PROVERBS 21:23

Do not speak in the ears of a fool for he will despise the wisdom of your words.

PROVERBS 23:9

As one who takes away a garment in cold weather, or vinegar on soda, so is one who sings songs to a heavy heart.

PROVERBS 25:20

Do not answer a fool according to his folly, lest you also be like him.

PROVERBS 26:4

Answer a fool according to his folly, lest he be wise in his own eyes.

PROVERBS 26:5

Do you see a man who is hasty in his words? There is more hope for a fool than for him.

PROVERBS 29:20

GOSSIP

The words of a gossip are like tasty morsels and they go down into a person's innermost parts.

PROVERBS 18:8

He who goes about as a talebearer reveals secrets; therefore do not keep company with him who opens wide his lips.

PROVERBS 20:19

The north wind brings forth rain: so a backbiting tongue brings an angry face.

PROVERBS 25:23

Without wood a fire goes out. Without gossip, contention ceases.

PROVERBS 26:20

7 THINGS NOT TOLERATED BY THE LORD

There are seven things which the LORD hates which are an abomination to him:

1. *Haughty eyes.*
2. *A lying tongue.*
3. *Hands that shed innocent blood.*
4. *A heart that devises wicked schemes.*
5. *Feet that are swift in running to mischief.*
6. *A false witness who utters lies.*
7. *He who sows discord among brothers.*

PROVERBS 6:16-19

THE WORDS OF AGUR

The words of Agur the son of Jakeh, the oracle: the man says to Ithiel, to Ithiel and Ucal:

"Surely I am the most ignorant man and do not have a man's understanding. I have not learned wisdom, neither do I have the knowledge of the Holy One. Who has ascended up into heaven and descended? Who has gathered the wind in his fists? Who has bound the waters in his garment? Who has established every part of the earth? What is his name and what is his son's name, if you know?"

"Every word of God is flawless. He is a shield to those who take refuge in him. Do not add to his words, lest he reprove you and you be found a liar."

PROVERBS 30:1-6

RIGHTEOUS (GOOD) VS WICKED (EVIL)

But the path of the righteous is like the dawning light that shines more and more until the perfect day. The way of the wicked is like darkness. They do not know what they stumble over.

PROVERBS 4:18-19

The LORD will not allow the soul of the righteous to go hungry but he thrusts away the desire of the wicked.

PROVERBS 10:3

Blessings are on the head of the righteous but violence covers the mouth of the wicked.

PROVERBS 10:6

The memory of the righteous is blessed but the name of the wicked will rot.

PROVERBS 10:7

The labor of the righteous leads to life. The increase of the wicked leads to sin.

PROVERBS 10:16

The tongue of the righteous is like choice silver. The heart of the wicked is of little worth.

PROVERBS 10:20

The lips of the righteous feed many but the foolish die for lack of understanding.

PROVERBS 10:21

What the wicked fear, will overtake them, but the desire of the righteous will be granted.

PROVERBS 10:24

When the whirlwind passes, the wicked is no more; but the righteous stand firm forever.

PROVERBS 10:25

The prospect of the righteous is joy but the hope of the wicked will perish.

PROVERBS 10:28

The righteous will never be removed but the wicked will not dwell in the land.

PROVERBS 10:30

The mouth of the righteous brings forth wisdom but the perverse tongue will be cut off.

PROVERBS 10:31

The lips of the righteous know what is acceptable but the mouth of the wicked is perverse.

PROVERBS 10:32

The integrity of the upright shall guide them but the perverseness of the treacherous shall destroy them.

PROVERBS 11:3

The righteousness of the upright shall deliver them but the unfaithful will be trapped by evil desires.

PROVERBS 11:6

When a wicked man dies, hope perishes, and expectation of power comes to nothing.

PROVERBS 11:7

A righteous person is delivered out of trouble and the wicked takes his place.

PROVERBS 11:8

With his mouth the godless man destroys his neighbor but the righteous will be delivered through knowledge.

PROVERBS 11:9

When it goes well with the righteous, the city rejoices. When the wicked perish, there is shouting.

PROVERBS 11:10

By the blessing of the upright, the city is exalted, but it is overthrown by the mouth of the wicked.

PROVERBS 11:11

Wicked people earn deceitful wages but one who sows righteousness reaps a sure reward.

PROVERBS 11:18

Most certainly, the evil man will not be unpunished, but the descendants of the righteous will be delivered.

PROVERBS 11:21

The desire of the righteous is only good. The expectation of the wicked is wrath.

PROVERBS 11:23

People curse someone who withholds grain but blessing will be on the head of him who sells it.

PROVERBS 11:26

The fruit of the righteous is a tree of life and he who plucks that life is wise.

PROVERBS 11:30

If the righteous is delivered with difficulty, where will the ungodly and the sinner appear?

PROVERBS 11:31

A good man shall obtain favor from the LORD but he will condemn a man of wicked devices.

PROVERBS 12:2

The words of the wicked are about lying in wait for blood but the speech of the upright rescues them.

PROVERBS 12:6

The wicked are overthrown, and are no more, but the house of the righteous shall stand.

PROVERBS 12:7

A righteous man regards the life of his animal but the tender mercies of the wicked are cruel.

PROVERBS 12:10

The wicked desires the plunder of evil men but the root of the righteous flourishes.

PROVERBS 12:12

An evil man is trapped by sinfulness of lips but the righteous shall come out of trouble.

PROVERBS 12:13

No mischief shall happen to the righteous but the wicked shall be filled with evil.

PROVERBS 12:21

A righteous person is cautious in friendship but the way of the wicked leads them astray.

PROVERBS 12:26

In the way of righteousness is life; in its path there is no death.

PROVERBS 12:28

By the fruit of his lips, a man enjoys good things; but the unfaithful crave violence.

PROVERBS 13:2

Righteousness guards the way of integrity but wickedness overthrows the sinner.

PROVERBS 13:6

The light of the righteous shines brightly but the lamp of the wicked is snuffed out.

PROVERBS 13:9

Misfortune pursues sinners but prosperity rewards the righteous.

PROVERBS 13:21

A good man leaves an inheritance to his children's children but the wealth of the sinner is stored for the righteous.

PROVERBS 13:22

The righteous one eats to the satisfying of his soul but the belly of the wicked goes hungry.

PROVERBS 13:25

The house of the wicked will be destroyed but the tent of the upright will flourish.

PROVERBS 14:11

The unfaithful will be repaid for his own ways; likewise a good man will be rewarded for his ways.

PROVERBS 14:14

Do they not go astray who plot evil? But love and faithfulness belong to those who plan good.

PROVERBS 14:22

The wicked is brought down in his calamity but the righteous has a refuge in his death.

PROVERBS 14:32

Righteousness exalts a nation but sin is a disgrace to any people.

PROVERBS 14:34

The heart of the righteous weighs answers but the mouth of the wicked gushes out evil.

PROVERBS 15:28

The LORD has made everything for its own end — yes, even the wicked for the day of evil.

PROVERBS 16:4

The highway of the upright is to depart from evil. He who keeps his way preserves his soul.

PROVERBS 16:17

A worthless man devises mischief. His speech is like a scorching fire.

PROVERBS 16:27

A perverse man stirs up strife and a gossip separates close friends.

PROVERBS 16:28

One who winks his eyes to plot perversities, one who compresses his lips, is bent on evil.

PROVERBS 16:30

Gray hair is a crown of glory. It is found in the path of righteousness.

PROVERBS 16:31

An evildoer heeds wicked lips. A liar gives ear to a mischievous tongue.

PROVERBS 17:4

An evil man seeks only rebellion; therefore a cruel messenger shall be sent against him.

PROVERBS 17:11

Whoever rewards evil for good, evil shall not depart from his house.

PROVERBS 17:13

He who justifies the wicked, and he who condemns the righteous, both of them alike are an abomination to the LORD.

PROVERBS 17:15

One who has a perverse heart doesn't find prosperity and one who has a deceitful tongue falls into trouble.

PROVERBS 17:20

The name of the LORD is a strong tower; the righteous run into it and are safe.

PROVERBS 18:10

A corrupt witness mocks justice and the mouth of the wicked gulps down iniquity.

PROVERBS 19:28

A king who sits on the throne of judgment scatters away all evil with his eyes.

PROVERBS 20:8

A high look, and a proud heart, the lamp of the wicked, is sin.

PROVERBS 21:4

The violence of the wicked will drive them away, because they refuse to do what is right.

PROVERBS 21:7

The soul of the wicked desires evil; his neighbor finds no mercy in his eyes.

PROVERBS 21:10

The Righteous One considers the house of the wicked and brings the wicked to ruin.

PROVERBS 21:12

It is joy to the righteous to do justice but it is a destruction to evildoers.

PROVERBS 21:15

The wicked is a ransom for the righteous; the treacherous for the upright.

PROVERBS 21:18

A wicked man hardens his face but as for the upright, he establishes his ways.

PROVERBS 21:29

Thorns and snares are in the path of the wicked: whoever guards his soul stays from them.

PROVERBS 22:5

The father of the righteous has great joy. Whoever fathers a wise child delights in him.

PROVERBS 23:24

Like a muddied spring and a polluted well, so is a righteous man who gives way before the wicked.

PROVERBS 25:26

The wicked flee when no one pursues but the righteous are as bold as a lion.

PROVERBS 28:1

Those who forsake the Law praise the wicked but those who keep the Law contend with them.

PROVERBS 28:4

Evil men do not understand justice but those who seek the LORD understand it fully.

PROVERBS 28:5

When the wicked rise, men hide themselves but when they perish, the righteous thrive.

PROVERBS 28:28

The righteous is concerned about justice for the poor. The wicked does not understand the concern.

PROVERBS 29:7

The bloodthirsty hate a man of integrity and they seek the life of the upright.

PROVERBS 29:10

When the wicked increase, sin increases but the righteous will see their downfall.

PROVERBS 29:16

A dishonest man detests the righteous and the upright in their ways detest the wicked.

PROVERBS 29:27

IN PRAISE OF WISDOM

Doesn't wisdom cry out? Doesn't understanding raise her voice? On the top of high places by the way, where the paths meet, she stands. Beside the gates, at the entry of the city, at the entry doors, she cries aloud: "To you men, I call. I send my voice to the sons of mankind. You simple, understand prudence. You fools, be of an understanding heart. Hear, for I will speak excellent things. The opening of my lips is for right things.

For my mouth speaks truth. Wickedness is an abomination to my lips. All the words of my mouth are in righteousness. There is nothing crooked or perverse in them. They are all plain to him who understands, right to those who find knowledge. Receive my instruction rather than silver; knowledge rather than choice gold. For wisdom is better than rubies. All the things that may be desired can't be compared to it."

"I, wisdom, have made prudence my dwelling. Find out knowledge and discretion. The fear of the LORD is to hate evil. I hate pride, arrogance, the evil way, and the perverse mouth. Counsel and sound knowledge are mine. I have understanding and power. By me kings reign and rulers decree justice. By me princes rule; nobles and all the righteous rulers of the earth. I love those who love me. Those who seek me diligently will find me.

With me are riches, honor, enduring wealth and prosperity.
My fruit is better than gold, yes, than fine gold; my yield
than choice silver. I walk in the way of righteousness, in the
midst of the paths of justice; that I may give wealth to those
who love me. I fill their treasuries."

"Now therefore, son, listen to me, for blessed are those who
keep my ways. Hear instruction and be wise. Do not refuse
it. Blessed is the man who hears me, watching daily at my
gates, waiting at my doorposts. For whoever finds me, finds
life and will obtain favor from the LORD. But he who sins
against me wrongs his own soul. All those who hate me love
death."

PROVERBS 8:1-21, 32-36

How much better it is to get wisdom than gold. Yes, to get
understanding is to be chosen rather than silver.

PROVERBS 16:16

THE REWARDS OF WISDOM

Wisdom has built her house. She has set up her seven pillars. She has prepared her meat. She has mixed her wine. She has also set her table. She has sent out her maidens. She cries from the highest places of the city: "Whoever is simple, let him turn in here." As for him who is void of understanding, she says to him, "Come, eat some of my bread, drink some of the wine which I have mixed. Leave your simple ways and live. Walk in the way of understanding."

He who corrects a mocker invites insult. He who reproves a wicked man invites abuse. Do not reprove a scoffer, lest he hate you. Reprove a wise man and he will love you. Instruct a wise man and he will be still wiser. Teach a righteous man and he will increase in learning. The fear of the LORD is the beginning of wisdom.

The knowledge of the Holy One is understanding. For by me your days will be multiplied. The years of your life will be increased. If you are wise, you are wise for yourself. If you mock, you alone will bear it. The foolish woman is loud, undisciplined and knows nothing. She sits at the door of her house, on a seat in the high places of the city, to call to those who pass by, who go straight on their ways, "Whoever is simple, let him turn in here." as for him who is void of understanding, she says to him, "Stolen water is sweet. Food eaten in secret is pleasant." But he doesn't know that the dead are there, that her guests are in the depths of Sheol.

PROVERBS 9:1-18

Listen, sons, to a father's instruction. Pay attention and know understanding; for I give you sound learning. Do not forsake my law. For I was a son to my father, tender and an only child in the sight of my mother. He taught me and said to me: "Let your heart retain my words. Keep my commandments and live. Get wisdom. Get understanding. Do not forget, neither swerve from the words of my mouth. Do not forsake her and she will preserve you. Love her and she will keep you.

Wisdom is supreme. Get wisdom. Yes, though it costs all your possessions, get understanding. Esteem her and she will exalt you. She will bring you to honor, when you embrace her. She will give to your head a garland of grace. She will deliver a crown of splendor to you." Listen, my son and receive my sayings. The years of your life will be many. I have taught you in the way of wisdom. I have led you in straight paths.

When you go, your steps will not be hampered. When you run, you will not stumble. Take firm hold of instruction. Do not let her go. Keep her, for she is your life. Do not enter into the path of the wicked. Do not walk in the way of evil men. Avoid it and do not pass by it. Turn from it and pass on. For they do not sleep, unless they do evil. Their sleep is taken away, unless they make someone fall. For they eat the bread of wickedness and drink the wine of violence.
But the path of the righteous is like the dawning light, that shines more and more until the perfect day. The way of the wicked is like darkness. They do not know what they stumble over.

My son, attend to my words. Turn your ear to my sayings. Let them not depart from your eyes. Keep them in the midst of your heart.

For they are life to him who finds them and health to all of his body. Guard your heart with all diligence, for out of it is the wellspring of life. Put away from yourself a perverse mouth. Put corrupt lips far from you. Let your eyes look straight ahead. Fix your gaze directly before you. Make the path of your feet level. Let all of your ways be established. Do not turn to the right hand nor to the left. Remove your foot from evil.

PROVERBS 4:1-27

WHAT DID YOU THINK ABOUT PROVERBS WITH GOD'S WISDOM?

Thank you for purchasing this book. I know you could have picked any number of books to read but you picked this book and for that I am extremely grateful.

I hope it added value and quality to your everyday life. If so, it would be really nice if you could share this book with your friends and family by posting to Facebook and Twitter.

If you enjoyed this book and found some benefit in reading it, I'd like to hear from you and hope that you could take some time to post a review on Amazon & Goodreads.

I want you to know that your review is very important to me.

Thank you again & I wish you all the best as you journey wisely through life.

ANOTHER BOOK TO CONSIDER

Psalms with God's Wisdom: Navigate life wisely with 100+ quotes & proverbs of wisdom, prayer, thanksgiving, trust, praise & worship hymns from the Biblical book of Psalms

Made in the USA
San Bernardino, CA
08 December 2019